Birdsong

RUMI

Birdsong

Fifty-three Short Poems
translated by Coleman Barks

MAYPOP   Athens, Georgia

COVER: The bird, its crown and neckband, compose the Bismillah, "In the Name of God, the Most Merciful, the Most Compassionate," written in thuluth script. The medallion behind the figure, and on the back cover, decorates one of the domes of Hagia Sophia in Istanbul. Its inscription is from the *Qur'an*, the sura entitled "Light." (XXIV, 35) The bird calligraphy dates from the 19th Century. The medallion from the 16th. Both images are found in Y. H. Safadi's *Islamic Calligraphy* (Shambhala, 1979).

ISBN 0-9618916-7-X

MAYPOP
196 Westview Drive
Athens, GA 30606

Set in Monotype PostScript Centaur & Arrighi
by Moreland Hogan in Charlotte, North Carolina.
Printed by Thomson-Shore, Inc., in Dexter, Michigan.

for Alexa

Contents

Introduction

The *rubai*,* the four-line poem, is indigenous to the Persian language, and Rumi is one of the great innovators with the form. There's a legend about how the quatrain originated. It's fair day. A poet and his friends are strolling along in the crowd. They stop to watch some children playing a game. A young boy throws a walnut so that it starts along a groove of the pavement, jumps out, then rolls back in to hit the aimed-at spot. He has put english on the nut, and he celebrates the move with a little chant. "Rolling, rolling, off and back, then home to the bottom of the ditch."

The poet (one version says it was Rudaki in the 10th Century) heard a new rhythm in the boy's elation, repeated it with slight differences three times, and thus the Persian quatrain was born! There is that spontaneous dance, and walnutty compression, in Rumi's short poems. The amazing variety, the playfulness of modes, does remind one of birdsong.

All the great mystical traditions love birds and their singing. Solomon understood what the different bird species were saying. That's why they loved to stay close around him. Jesus, playing as a child, made clay birds on the sabbath, and when scolded, shooed them into flight, his first miracle. Taoist grave carvings sometimes show one master handing a bird to another master, or a wonderfully strange procession of birds and bird-people strutting in high spirits into the next reality. St. Francis was so empty of nervous haste and fear and aggression that the birds would light on him.

Birds represent our longings for purity and freedom, and they carry messages of ineffable joy. They mediate between above and below. Some of them begin at dawn to celebrate the returning light. And some with their songs in the middle of the night deepen our silence. I have seen a television documentary about how Canary Islanders have a human whistling language that they use to call information across the cliffs. "The mailboat is in!" "The priest is not feeling well. No mass this afternoon." It's not the same. I don't mean to sentimentalize the birds here, but simply to acknowledge what Wallace Stevens called their "sweet questioning" of reality, the morning meadow talk.

Walking an Irish hillside once, I was stunned, as everyone is, by the performance of a skylark. Falling-warbling, a chunked gob of pure kamakazi watermusic, unbelieveably fluid and beyond any melody. Poets never achieve the skylark's free-fall, but they aspire, especially in short poems, to the condition.

But what is this fountain of sound? What are the birds doing? One of the loveliest scientific ideas that I know of is Rudolf Steiner's understanding of how plants are part of sonic systems, responding subtly to swallow wingbeats, pre-dawn warbling, and the flamboyant swamp-choruses of the peepers. Certain sounds waken cellular functions. Minute mouthlike openings called *stomata*, for example, which plants use to exchange various aerosols and mists with the surrounding atmosphere, seem to be triggered by a combination of musical frequencies and harmonics. The birds are helping the plants! Recent researchers have found that Vivaldi, some Indian raga melodies, and Bach's E-major concerto for the violin also stimulate cells to action. We intuitively hope and feel that this is true. Birdsong and Bach and the longing of the sitar *should* be meshing with the mysteries of seed germination and plant growth. O let the poems we say plump out the peaches!

These unifying metaphors, or facts, are certainly not foreign to Rumi's vision of the dance.

> Every forest branch moves differently
> in the breeze, but as they sway,
> they connect at the roots.

> — COLEMAN BARKS
> Feb. 28, 1993

* These translations have been re-worked from A. J. Arberry's volume, *The Rubaiyat of Jalal al-din Rumi, Select translations into English verse,* Emery Walker, Ltd. (London, 1949).

Birdsong

Birdsong brings relief
to my longing.

I am just as ecstatic as they are,
but with nothing to say!

Please, universal soul, practice
some song, or something, through me!

The way of love is not
a subtle argument.

The door there
is devastation.

Birds make great sky-circles
of their freedom.
How do they learn it?

They fall, and falling,
they're given wings.

Let your throat-song
be clear and strong enough

to make an emperor fall full-length,
suppliant, at the door.

I have phrases and whole pages memorized,
but nothing can be told of love.

You must wait until you and I
are living together.

In the conversation we'll have
then . . . be patient . . . then.

Sometimes I call you wine, or cup,
sunlight ricocheting off those,
or faintly immersed in silver.

I call you trap and bait,
and the game I'm after, all
so as not to say your name.

I was happy enough to stay still
inside the pearl inside the shell,

but the hurricane of experience
lashed me out of hiding and made me

a wave moving into shore, saying loudly
the ocean's secret as I went, and then

spent there, I slept like fog against
the cliff, another stillness.

I used to have fiery intensity,
and a flowing sweetness.

The waters were illusion.
The flames, made of snow.

Was I dreaming then?
Am I awake now?

I run around looking for the Friend.
My life is almost over,
but I'm still asleep!

When it happens, if it happens,
that I meet the Friend,
will I get the lost years back?

We search this world for the great untying
of what was wed to us with birth
and gets undone at dying.

We sleep beside a stream, thirsty.
Cursed and unlucky his whole life,

an old man finishes up in a niche
of a ruin, inches from the treasure!

There is a desert
I long to be walking,
a wide emptiness,

peace beyond any
understanding of it.

When the soul first put on the body's shirt,
the ocean lifted up all its gifts.

When love first tasted the lips
of being human, it started singing.

Slave, be aware that the Lord
of all the East is here.

A flickering stormcloud
shows his lightnings to you!

Your words are guesswork.
He speaks from experience.
There's a huge difference!

Which is worth more, a crowd of thousands,
or your own genuine solitude?
Freedom, or power over an entire nation?

A little while alone in your room
will prove more valuable than anything else
that could ever be given you.

I saw grief drinking a cup of sorrow
and called out,
             "It tastes sweet,
does it not?"
             "You've caught me,"
grief answered,
             "and you've ruined my business.
How can I sell sorrow,
             when you know it's a blessing?"

Love lit a fire in my chest, and anything
that wasn't love left: intellectual
subtlety, philosophy
books, school.

All I want now
to do or hear
is poetry.

Love is that that never sleeps,
nor even rests, nor stays
for long with those that do.

Love is language
that cannot be said,
or heard.

With your lips not here
I kiss rubies to remember.

When I can't sip from you,
I put my lip on the cup's lip.

Instead of reaching
into your sky, I kneel
and take handfuls of earth.

Be fair. Admit that love has in it
all the righteousness we need.

Confess that you're willing to forget
and be numb enough to call some
low desire a holy name.

Live as evidence
that there is a way
from wanting to longing.

You're from a country beyond this universe,
yet your best guess is
you're made of earth and ashes!

You engrave this physical image everywhere
as a sign that you've forgotten
where you're from!

Essence is emptiness.
Everything else, accidental.

Emptiness brings peace to your loving.
Everything else, disease.

In this world of trickery emptiness
is what your soul wants.

We're not afraid of God's blade,
or of being chained up, or
of having our heads severed.

We're burning up quickly, tasting
a little hellfire as we go.

You cannot imagine
how little it matters to us
what people say.

Come to this street with
only your sweet fragrance.

Don't walk into *this* river
wearing a robe!

Paths go from here to there,
but don't arrive from somewhere!
It's time now to live naked.

Soul serves as a cup for the juice
that leaves the intellect in ruins.

That candle came and consumed me,
about whose flame the universe
flutters in total confusion.

The mystic dances in the sun,
hearing music others don't.

"Insanity," they say, those others.
If so, it's a very gentle,
nourishing sort.

This love is beyond the range of language,
but you come in asking, "How's your heart?"

holding your robe up slightly.
I answer, "Hold it higher!

This slaughterhouse floor
is running with blood."

I want to be where
your bare foot walks,

because maybe before you step,
you'll look at the ground.
I want that blessing.

Would you like to have revealed to you
the truth of the Friend?

Leave the rind,
and descend into the pith.

Fold within fold, the Beloved
drowns in his own being. This world
is drenched with that drowning.

Love perfected and whole, you arrive.
Words throng my soul, but none come out.

A traveler meets his joy
and his despair at once.

Dying of thirst, I stand here
with springwater flowing around my feet.

Spring overall. But inside us
there's another unity.

Behind each eye here,
one glowing weather.

Every forest branch moves differently
in the breeze, but as they sway
they connect at the roots.

A drunk saw me coming and clapped his hands,
"Look here! Our pilgrim's come back!
Against all his repentence vows."

It was true, but he didn't know much
about glassmaking, the painstaking work.

Remember: the more effort goes in,
the easier we are to break.

Rain fell on one man,
he ran into his house.

But the swan spread its wings and said,
"Pour more on me of that power
I was fashioned from."

Around and around all night
in the house of the Friend,

this is how it must be,
because the Beloved needs
the cup empty, again empty.

What's the lover to do,
but humiliate himself,
and wander your rooms?

If he kisses your hair,
don't wonder why.

Sometimes in the madhouse
they gnaw on their chains.

Last night, the Friend
came to visit.

I asked night
to keep the secret.

"But look!" said night,
"Behind you, and over there
the sun is rising!

How could I show
anyone anything?"

My spirit saw how dull and down
I was and came and sat laughing

on my bed. Holding my brow,
"Sweetheart, I can't bear
to see you like this!"

This is how I would die
into the love I have for you:

as pieces of cloud
dissolve in sunlight.

Someone who does not run
toward the allure of love
walks a road where nothing

lives. But this dove here
senses the love-hawk floating
above, and waits, and will not

be driven or scared to safety.

Flowers open every night
across the sky as the peace

of keeping a vigil
kindles the emptiness.

Don't for a moment think that you've found
the goal of your love! Don't stand still
in the ranks. You have no place
with uniforms at rest.

You might as well consent to be a corsage,
or a rose in some beautiful woman's hair.

A road might end at a single house,
but it's not love's road.

Love is a river.
Drink from it.

One who does what the Friend wants done
will never need a friend.

There's bankruptcy that's pure gain.
The moon stays bright when it
doesn't avoid the night.

A rose's rarest essence
lives in the thorn.

A lightwind coming downhill,
the nightbird's song.

The strange writing I read
on my lover's door

says the same message
now being called out
over the rooftops.

My memory of your face
prevents my seeing you.

Lightning veils your brow.
Recalling our kissing,
I can't kiss you now.

So strange, such sweetness
could keep us apart.

Your fragrance fills the meadow.
Your mouth appears in a red anemone,

but when those reminders leave,
my own lips open,
and in whatever I say,
I hear you.

How long are you going to beat me
like a drum and make me sigh
for you like a violin.

You answer, "Come. I'll hold you close
and stroke you like a lute."

But I feel more like a flute
that you put in your mouth
and then neglect to blow.

I realize that the dawn
when we'll meet again
will never break,

so I give it up,
little by little, this love.

But something in me laughs
as I say this, someone

shaking his head and chuckling
softly, *Hardly, hardly.*

A bird delegation came to Solomon complaining,
"Why is it you never criticize the nightingale?"

"Because my way," the nightingale explained
for Solomon, "is different. Mid-March
to mid-June I sing. The other

nine months, while you
continue chirping,
I'm silent."

You thought union was a way
you could decide to go.

But the world of the soul follows
things rejected and almost forgotten.

Your true guide drinks
from an undammed stream.

This mud-body
is clear epiphany.

Angels wish they
could move as I move.

Purity? Cherubim babies
long for my innocence.

Courage? Armies of demons
flee my uplifted hand.

Spring paints the countryside.
Cypress trees grow even more beautiful,
but let's stay inside.

Lock the door.
Come to me naked.
No one's here.

How will you know the difficulties
of being human, if you're always
flying off to blue perfection?

Where will you plant your grief-seeds?
Workers need ground to scrape and hoe,
not the sky of unspecified desire.

Rise. Move around the center
as pilgrims wind the Kaaba.

Being still is how one clay clod
sticks to another in sleep,

while movement wakes us up
and unlocks new blessings.

You walk in looking like you're about to say,
"Enough of this!" But it'll take more

than frowns and harsh talking
to make my love leave.

This is the undauntable bird,
who's never been caged,
or felt fear.

Imagining is like feeling around
in a dark lane, or washing
your eyes with blood.

You *are* the truth
from foot to brow. Now,
what else would you like to know?

You that come to birth and bring the mysteries,
your voice-thunder makes us very happy.

Roar, lion of the heart,
and tear me open.

Love swells and surges the ocean
and on your robe of stormcloud
sews rain designs.

Love is lightning,
and also the *ahhh*
we respond with.

Pale sunlight,
pale the wall.

Love moves away.
The light changes.

I need more grace
than I thought.

In your light I learn how to love.
In your beauty, how to make poems.

You dance inside my chest,
where no one sees you,

but sometimes I do, and that
sight becomes this art.

You're the spring.
We're grasses trailing in it.

You're the king coming by.
We're beggars along the road.

You're the voice
we're echoes of.

You're calling for us now.
How could we not return?

Lovers in their brief delight
gamble both worlds away,
a century's worth of work
for one chance to surrender.

Many slow growth-stages build
to quick bursts of blossom.

A thousand half-loves
must be forsaken to take
one whole heart home.

You that prefer, like crows do,
winter's chill and the empty limbs,

notice now this that fills
with new leaves and roses opening
and the nightbird's song.

Let your love dissolve also
into *this* season's moment,

or when it's over, you'll buy
lamp after lamp to find it!

Drumsound rises on the air,
its throb, my heart.

A voice inside the beat
says, "I know you're tired,
but come. This is the way."

Stars burn clear
all night till dawn.

Do that yourself, and a spring
will rise in the dark with water
your deepest thirst is for.

Don't sleep now. Let the turning
night wheel through this circle.

Your brow, the moon, this
lantern we sit with.

Stay awake with these
lights. Don't sleep.

If you want what visible reality
can give, you're an employee.

If you want the unseen world,
you're not living your truth.

Both wishes are foolish,
but you'll be forgiven for forgetting
that what you really want is
love's confusing joy.

Gamble everything for love,
if you're a true human being.

If not, leave
this gathering.

Half-heartedness doesn't reach
into majesty. You set out
to find God, but then you keep

stopping for long periods
at meanspirited roadhouses.

In a boat down a fast-running creek,
it feels like trees on the bank
are rushing by. What seems

to be changing around us
is rather the speed of our craft
leaving this world.

What is this that gives pleasure
in a form, then when not,
turns dull, opaque?

This thing that slips away
into infinity, then strikes
down to take another shape?

I said, "I will lift from your hand
like a pigeon." You said,

"It will be my love
that opens your wings."

I said, "Totally humble, like a dog
I'll lay down by your feet."

"Such glory for you!"
you said.

The soul must suffer secrets
that can't be said, public humiliation,
people pointing in contempt.

While you are a human being,
stay inside the scorn. Work there
patiently with the others.

When you're pure spirit,
quickly, leave!

Love is the way messengers
from the mystery tell us things.

Love is the mother.
We are her sons.

She shines inside us,
visible-invisible, as we trust
or lose trust, or feel it start to grow again.

Childhood, youth and maturity,
and now old age.

Every guest agrees to stay
three days, no more.

Master, you told me to
remind you. Time to go.

Are you jealous of the ocean's generosity?
Why would you refuse to give
this joy to anyone?

Fish don't hold the sacred liquid in cups.
They swim the huge fluid freedom.

Lo I am with you always,
you promised that,
and when I realized it was true,
my soul flared up.

Any unhappiness comes from forgetting.
Remember, and be back close
with the Friend.

There is a banquet where grains of wheat
sit and eat and shout for more,
and more is brought.

These banqueter seed-grains never
quit eating, and for eternity
the table stays replete.

You've so distracted me,
your absence fans my love.
Don't ask how.

Then you come near.
"Do not . . . ," I say, and
"Do not . . . ," you answer.

Don't ask why
this delights me.

Real value comes with madness,
matzub below, scientist above.

Whoever finds love
beneath hurt and grief

disappears into emptiness
with a thousand new disguises.

A bough with blossoms bears fruit.
The hawk descends with purpose.

Your image comes and goes here
inside me. When will you stay?

Poem, song, and story,
the stream sweeps by, moving along
what was never mine anyway.

What I've done through an act of will,
well-meaning or mean, these are brought in
briefly by moonlight and carried obscurely off.

Roses shine in the clay
beside your tomb.

Be aware, earth,
who sleeps inside you!

Spring lightning, poems
being sung. The drum

gets quiet, but
voices continue.

Venus appears, bringing
her gift to the music.

This season with the Friend so near,
the body dims. Heart-light
grows more intense.

Stormclouds finally weep, because
the lightning has started to laugh.

With heavy tears everywhere coming down,
the fields get uncontrollably tickled.

The angel of death arrives,
and I spring joyfully up.

No one knows what comes over me
when I and that messenger speak!

When you come back inside my chest,
no matter how far I've wandered off,
I look around and see the way.

At the end of my life, with just one breath
left, if you come then, I'll sit up and sing.

I called through your door,
"The mystics are gathering
in the street. Come out!"

"Leave me alone.
I'm sick."

"I don't care if you're dead!
Jesus is here, and he wants
to resurrect somebody!"

All our lives we've looked
into each other's faces.
That was the case today too.

How do we keep our love-secret?
We speak from brow to brow
and hear with our eyes.

Last night things flowed between us
that cannot now be said or written.

Only as I'm being carried out
and down the road, as the folds
of my shroud open in the wind,

will anyone be able to read, as on
the petal-pages of a turning bud
what passed through us last night.

When I remember your love,
I weep, and when I hear people
talking of you,
            something in my chest,
where nothing much happens now,
moves as in sleep.

As essence turns to ocean,
the particles glisten.

Watch how in this candleflame instant
blaze all the moments you have lived.

There is a way of breathing
that's a shame and suffocation.

And there's another way of expiring,
a love-breath that lets you open infinitely.

Lovers gather and give each other shade,
relief from the direct sun.

Stay closeby that community.
Be shade with them, until you yourself
are full of light like the moon, then like the sun.

The rose took from another presence
its crimson grace, as a thief
on the gallows takes the breeze.

So the nightingale begs all night,
to no avail, the morning air,
"Warn of what you bring!"

Whoever loves, loves
the same sweetheart I do.

Lightning, there and there,
comes from one turning jewel.

Before creation, gold was stamped
with a seal, so now no matter
where it hides in the ground,
it belongs to me!

You're in my eyes.
How else could I see light?

You're in my brain.
This wild joy.

If love did not live in matter,
how would any place have
any hold on anyone?

Don't analyze this enthusiasm!

The wheel that lifts some up
and drags others down,
we're not riding it anymore.

We've jumped off that
good-and-bad.

If you want money more than anything,
you'll be bought and sold.

If you have a greed for food,
you'll be a loaf of bread.

This is a subtle truth:
whatever you love, you are.

You're not a slave.
You're a king.

If you *want* something,
release the wish and let it light
on its desire, completely free of the personal.

Then sit and sound the drum
of nothing, nothing.

The first morning air brings
the presence that angels
in amazement watch.

Tears and a breathing silence
together. Then the morning itself,
growing stronger, calls out,

"Who's loving who,
of these two?"

I claimed my eyes.

"I'll join them to the river
in rainy season."
                    "My loving."
"Blood-red."
              "But at least my body
is mine!"
          "Before just a few days go by,
people will point at it and sneer
and drive you out of town."

I placed one foot on the wide plain
of death, and some grand
immensity sounded on the emptiness.

I have felt nothing ever
like the wild wonder of that moment.

I used to be shy.
You made me sing.

I used to refuse things at table.
Now I shout for more wine.

In somber dignity, I used to sit
on my mat and pray.

Now children run through
and make faces at me.

People want you to be happy.
Don't keep serving them your pain!

If you could untie your wings
and free your soul of jealousy,

you and everyone around you
would fly up like doves.

Translations Available from Maypop

These translations were done by Coleman Barks in collaboration with the Persian scholar, John Moyne, Head of Linguistics, City University of New York, and with other scholarly sources listed in the various volumes.

RUMI

Open Secret (Threshold, 1984)—83pp. $9.00. A selection of odes, quatrains, and selections from the *Mathnawi*, with Introduction. Winner of a Pushcart Writer's Choice Award. William Stafford, judge.

Unseen Rain (Threshold, 1986)—83pp. $9.00. One hundred and fifty short poems from Rumi's *Rubaiyat*, with Introduction.

We Are Three (Maypop, 1987)—87pp. $7.50. Odes, quatrains, and sections from the *Mathnawi*, with Notes.

These Branching Moments (Copper Beech, 1988)—52pp. $6.95. Forty odes, with Introduction.

This Longing (Threshold, 1988)—107pp. $9.00. Sections from the *Mathnawi* and from the *Letters*, with Introductions.

Delicious Laughter (Maypop, 1989)—128pp. $7.50. Rambunctious teaching stories and other more lyric sections from the *Mathnawi*, with Introduction and Notes.

Like This (Maypop, 1989)—68pp. $7.50. Forty-three odes from the *Divani Shamsi Tabriz*, with Introduction and Notes.

Feeling the Shoulder of the Lion (Threshold, 1991)—103pp. $9.00. Selections from the *Mathnawi*, with Introduction and Notes.

One-Handed Basket Weaving (Maypop, 1991)—135pp. $9.00. Selections from the *Mathnawi* on the theme of work, with Introduction, Notes, and Afterword.

LALLA

Naked Song, poems of a 14th century Kashmiri woman mystic, (Maypop, 1992)—80pp. $8.00.

SIXTH DALAI LAMA

Stallion on a Frozen Lake, love songs of the 17th century tantric master, (Maypop, 1992)—72pp. $8.00.

A volume of Coleman Barks' own writing is also now available, *Gourd Seed*, his poetry and short prose from the last fifteen years, (Maypop, 1993)—128pp. $9.00.

Order from Maypop: 1-800-682-8637. 196 Westview Drive, Athens, GA 30606. Postage and handling, $2.00 for the first, and $1.00 for each additional item.